STEPHEN M. JOSEPH was born in 1938 in New York and attended the public schools there. He received his bachelor's degree in English from Ohio State University in 1960, and has attended Mexico City College, Ohio University, and Hunter College. He now teaches in New York. He has edited several anthologies and is author of the novel, THE SHARK BITES BACK.

DIANE DAVIS
'69

THE ME NOBODY KNOWS;

Children's Voices from the Ghetto

edited by
Stephen M. Joseph

Acknowledgments

The editor has made every effort to trace the ownership of, and secure permission for, all copyrighted material in this volume. If any errors have inadvertently been made, proper corrections will be made in future editions. Thanks are due to *What's Happening?* for permission to use the following selections:

WHAT AM I?, I SPEAK IN AN ILLUSION, FROM EAST TO WEST, THE TRANSFORMATION, THE SLUM, I HATE PIGEONS, ON BROADWAY, THE STORY OF MY BLOCK, REJOICE, MUSINGS, A POEM (Beauty triumphs in the end of man . . .), A POEM (Another man has died . . .), WAR BABIES, A POEM (What happens to life . . .).

AVON BOOKS
A division of
The Hearst Corporation
959 Eighth Avenue
New York, New York 10019

Published by arrangement with the editor.

First Avon Printing, January, 1969

Cover illustration by Patricia Taylor

Printed in the U.S.A.

CONTENTS

To Barbara

INTRODUCTION

INTRODUCTION

The children whose writing appears in this book live in the slums. Their ages range from seven to eighteen and most of them are Black or Puerto Rican. There is a tendency to use words like "inner city" and "disadvantaged area," but the word slum to most people means poverty, dirt, and despair. Bedford-Stuyvesant, Harlem, Jamaica, and the lower west and east sides of Manhattan are slums, or ghettos.

These are not just poor neighborhoods. There is garbage in the streets and on the sidewalks, and often there are rusty hulks of burned-out cars, abandoned, their doors gaping open.

People in these neighborhoods resent the word slum; hearing it, they feel patronized, categorized, and put down.

My intention, in this book, is to diminish the stigma of this word by showing that these children of the ghetto, if given the chance and an open climate to write, have a tremendous amount to say and are anxious to speak.

The problem is that they often lack the means to say it. Their ability to write is not equal to their ideas—or so I thought.

This anthology resulted from my growing awareness that the children I had been teaching were something special. All children are.

It became important to me to make other people aware of this. I'm sure a great many people already know this and have known it for some time, but a great many more do not. This book is primarily for them and for the children and teachers whom I hope it will encourage to be freer in their writing and teaching.

I originally planned an anthology of writing from my classes alone, but I began to see that this might limit the scope of the book. I started to seek out teachers all over New York City who had been freely encouraging children to write. I learned that learning and fear are antithetical and that the techniques for teaching children must and do come out of an attitude about children and learning.

The children whose writing appears here trusted their teachers because the teachers were able to step outside of the punitive, authoritarian punishment and reward approach of our educational system.

Most of the teachers do not grade the children's writing. A low grade diminishes a child's interest in writing. He assumes he just didn't give the teacher what she wanted and he becomes discouraged. The idea is not to give the teacher what she wants, but for the child to feel he can write what **he** wants to write.

The children should feel free to speak without fear of being evaluated. In this context, neither punishment nor reward, represented by high or low grades, makes any sense. Evaluation focuses their attention on approval and not on exploring their ideas.

A teacher who insists on perfect spelling, micrometer margins, and neatness—in fact, a teacher who **insists** on anything—will get "What I Did Last Summer" and "We Should All Try To Be Good Citizens" essays, because insisting is just the thing not to do if you want someone to tell you how **he** feels. The more rigid the requirements, the more rigid the writing.

Discipline in writing can be a good thing if it is imposed from within. First the children need to see what it's like to really think on paper.

I ask only that the children's writing be clear enough for me to read. I've found that the need to master the mechanics and the craft of writing come later.

Most of these children have a rudimentary knowledge of how words go together. Most people never progress beyond this point because they are frozen into rigidity by all the strictures imposed upon them in school.

Children are anxious to learn the rules after they see that it's worth their while. Watch a bunch of kids playing softball or hide-and-go-seek. They often enjoy the form of the game as much as the content. But first they've learned that these games bring pleasure.

When I ask a new group of children to write, they almost always protest. When I ask them why they're groaning, they tell me they've been told they have to write a certain way: The "neatness counts" way, which makes writing a hard, unpleasant chore.

I talk to them about the differences and similarities between talking, singing, and playing the guitar. They are all ways of saying what you feel. So is writing. I ask them why most of them love to talk but hate to write. When they begin to tell me their answer to that question, I ask them to write it instead.

Sometimes I've told children they could write about anything they wanted to. Often this approach just draws blank stares and a lot of looking out the window.

Naomi Levinson is a teacher whose kids write all the time.

For the past seven years she has been helping children in the career guidance program at Junior High School 142—Queens to express themselves through writing. The children in this program have emotional problems and are hampered by low IQ's (70-90), low or non-existent reading scores and no experience in writing.

She puts one word on the blackboard, such a word as "Hope," or "Death," or "Love." Then she points to it and says **"Write."**

"What should we write?" the children ask.

"Can we write about . . ."

"You can write about anything the word I put on the board makes you think about. I'll help you with spelling if you feel you need help. Let's go!"

Many children feel threatened by not knowing how to spell. They can't begin to write if they feel they don't have the tools, so Naomi helps them spell.

This approach works for her because she's pro-child. She is for them, for anything that will make them more skilled, more able to cope with their problems, and they know it. Much of the writing in this book was written by her students.

Again, it's a matter of attitude; toward learning and toward children.

Here's what I do:

I tell the children I'd like them to write at least a page. I urge kids who don't want to write to try, but I don't force anyone.

I tell them that they have three choices. First, they can write about something that's important to them and sign their name. If they want me to, I'll discuss their writing with them at lunch or before or after school. Second, they can omit their names, but still hand the writing in to me. Third, they can write a page and neither sign their name nor hand it in.

I tell them they can take their writing with them if they think it's too personal to show to me. Once they've written, I've accomplished my goal of getting them to see their ideas on paper.

Most children respond. They write. Many children do take their writing with them when they leave, but some of the children who started writing with the idea of not signing their names decide they want to talk about their work with me, and they do sign their names.

Some of the children who meant to take their work with them also decide to give it to me to look at.

I feel that they trust me, for much of the writing is intensely personal. For this reason, and to avoid some of the complications that could arise in an anthology which includes the work of nearly 200 children, I've used initials except when I felt that I could use the children's names.

THE ME NOBODY KNOWS is divided into four sections. In the first, **How I See Myself,** the children write about their families, friends, and school, but mostly about how it feels to be lonely.

How I See My Neighborhood reflects the realities of poor urban areas all over America: dirt, drugs, and violence.

These children have fun, too, like kids anywhere. They ride their bikes, go to the movies, play records and dance, and sometimes they even join the Boy Scouts.

Fortunately, despair is not yet a refuge for these children, but this section reflects their growing anger and bewilderment.

These children see **The World Outside** mostly as a fantasy. Since they go to school in the ghetto and live in the ghetto, their primary contact with the outside world is through television and the movies.

They have fantasies about money, lots of money, and what they would buy and do with it. But they also see the world outside as a place where the sun freezes and rich people throw dollar bills in the air.

In **Things I Can't See or Touch,** the children write about love and sleep and about growing up. They talk about God, and hope and fear, and night and dying.

I've found that some kids will write what they think you want and some will put you on, but most of them write for keeps, because they need to, and because the talented and dedicated people who are their teachers made it possible for them to tell it like it is, or at least how it is to them.

Stephen M. Joseph
New York, 1968

HOW I SEE MYSELF

HOW I SEE MYSELF

In this section the children write about school, their families, their friends, and their loneliness.

One child writes about his first experiences with heroin. Others write about money; some write about grief; and there are some letters and journals from boys in reform school.

The mood of this section is questioning, wistful, and tentative, while the following sections reflect an increasing confusion and anger with life as seen from the ghetto.

Some of the work is funny, and meant to be, but most of it is serious. Akmir writes a fable about being turned into a fountain pen while working in a plastic factory. Another child writes a Dorian Gray fantasy in reverse: He gradually disappears and dies while looking in the mirror.

The children manifest a strong interest in the family; in having a family or longing for one.

Spenser Jameson is one of the teachers who helped me with this collection. He spent ten years teaching at the New York City Youth House, a "locked shelter." Boys and girls live there while the courts decide whether to send them home or to a training school.

Training schools used to be called reform schools.

The writing that the children did with Jameson included poems and short biographies. These children are not only literate, but talented.

According to Board of Education tests most of the children in Youth House are semi-literate. Many are considered illiterate.

Ed Grady is also a teacher at Youth House. He, and other teachers there, correspond with, visit, and often send gifts to former students who are now in State Training Schools.

One child writes, "I am trying to write what I see, not what I don't see."

As you'll see, they are all trying to write what they feel, not what they don't feel.

John W **Age 13**

Sometimes I feel as if somebody is always talking about me. I feel as if I weren't wanted. When I walk down the street, the kids are always yelling as they play.
There are also some dogs.

Gregory H **Age 13**

Sometimes I feel as if everybody is looking at me, I walk a little faster, I go out of my way just so I won't see everyone. The little kids yell out: "The fat pig is going by!" and everybody runs. When I get home my brother won't open the door because he says I can use my key.

Linda O **Age 13**

On a nice cold September morning, I got up and was afraid to go to school.

Ana **Age 8**

I wish that My farther will come back with My Mother. And I hope that whole world be peace and freedom.

the End

Victor Y **Age 13**

When I first get up in the morning I feel fresh and it seems like it would be a good day to me. But after I get in school, things change and they seem to turn into problems for me. And by the end of the day I don't even feel like I'm young. I feel tired.

Dennis F **Age 13**

MY ONE FATHER

I am 13 years old and my sisters, one of them is six and one of them is seven. And I do not know how old my father is because it was when I was a little baby, about three months old, when my father left; so I will tell you how old my mother is, around thirty-six. And I wish that my father would come back where he started at the beginning. I have been so lonesome with no one to play with or go out with.

My one father.

Isaac J **Age 13**

I am not like all the other children. I'm different because I like to hear birds singing but I don't like to hear people shouting. It is not nice to hear people yelling or shouting in the street.

Lorenzo **Age 8**

THE STORY OF MY LIFE

I was born at my house. I was born at my house because my mother did not get to the hospital on time. I was born in Pourto rico. My mother was married to my father. After that my mother went away to New Jursey. There she found my new father. He took me to age of 3. And then we came to new York. We lived in manhatin. And there they robed us. And then we moved to Stagg. There we had trouble with the landlord. we moved to Nicker Bocker. There we had to move because we have trouble with the water and the service. And from there we moved to Major. There we are having trouble with service and my father got in jail for a day. And there I stayed and went to school and hope that I'll never move.

Djangatolum (Lloyd Corbin) **Age 17**

STREETS '65-66

The horse, the horse
The evil white horse
Whose contents comes in grains
White sand of which I'm about to blow
To blow in my nose than into my veins
To unlatch my sub-conscious
To wash my convolutions bare
To rob my soul of the fiber
That was once there
Enslaving me to anger and despair
Freeing me of hope, happiness and
love's tender Kiss
For all it is to you, me, anyone
it is too much for one soul to bear
For all it is
For all it is to do
For all it is that I shall never do
For all it is to blow the white horse
That enters through my nose
And down my veins
To close my consciousness
To make cold the breast
that once warmed the rest

Unsigned **Age 16**

SUMMERTIME IN THE YOUTH HOUSE

I was in Youth House on the 4th of July. When I started thinking of the things that I could be doing, and the places I would be, I just got madder. As I was sitting down thinking to myself, my man Willie came over and we started talking about what we were going to do on the 4th of July. As we were talking, one of the supervisors came up to us and told us that there would be a lot of things going on, on the 4th of July. When me and Willie heard that, I had a grin on my face bigger than ever before. We couldn't wait for the 4th to come around. I had been in Youth House longer than Willie, so it meant more to me than it did to him. When the third came around, the Youth House gave out a list of activities. When the 4th of July came, I couldn't wait until everything started. The first thing we did was play the girls a game of baseball. Of course, we one. After the game I just sat around thinking about what I would be doing outside. I was thinking about last 4th of July, and what I did. I remember me and my brother and my friend. We all went to Coney Island. I didn't have too much money, but I had enough to do what I wanted to do that night. I went on just about all the rides. Then all of us went on the beach and played records and danced. I had a lot of fun that day and I don't think I will ever forget it. And now, here I was sitting on the grass, looking at the boys and girls playing, instead of sitting on the sand looking at the water and the people on the rides.

After thinking about the past, I got up, because we were getting ready to eat dinner. After dinner it started to rain.

M.B. **Age 16**

SUN

When children see you in the summer,
Sun-
        they like you.
They swim, laugh and play,
Sun-
        under your warmth.
But in winter,
sun-
        they lose their affection for you.
You melt their snow
sun-
        they dislike you.
But why
sun-
        must I always have winter?

Craig S Age 16

TO WHOM IT MAY CONCERN

I have seen the last of rising
suns
Because my death is soon to come.
I will no longer walk the sandy
shores
Or with my eyes the sky explore.
I've lived in this big bag of
tricks
And I have struggled to exist
But I am one of every fix
Whose mortal brain is so confused
That I don't know which way to
turn.
So while I waited my soul has
burned.
I have reached my destination's
peak.
No more adventures shall I seek.
So to discontinue my suffering
heart,
My love, my life, I shall depart.

I.F. **Age 16**

WHAT I LOVE

I love girls. I love what the girls have. I am nuts about the girls that are big and fine. All the girls love something about the boys and the boys love that thing that the girls got. It's so good to be with a girl in bed at night. Boy you don't sleep at night working and when morning come you have lost 10 pounds in bed. And your girl gained 10 pounds. Every boy losed pounds but we love that thing that girls have.

This girl was asked to write about what was important to her.

Unsigned **Age 12**

BOYS!

Boys, Boys, Boys, Boys, Boys,
Boys, Boys, Boys, Boys, Boys,
BOYS!!!

R.C. Age 16

BLACK

Black we die
Black you cry
Black I cry
Does White they cry
Cause Black we die?
Why they kill me?
What crime you and me?
Oh, yes! Now I see.
Black is our skin and
We want to be free.
Yes black we be
That they can see
Of you and me
But what of the soul
That yearns to be free?
This they do not see in
You or I
But this is that
This cannot die.

Unsigned **Age 13**

When my uncle died I was the lonely one. I not sleep and when I went to sleep I was dreaming about my uncle. At morning we went to see them and my mother was crying and some more people was too. In a week everybody was happy.

Benjamin Warrick **Age 14**

Sometimes I feel awful. When my mother is very very unhappy I try to find some way to cheer her up. When my father and mother get into a little fight it makes the whole house unhappy. Sometime some of us brake down and cry or go to our room. Some time I'd go to my friends house and asked her if she'd wanted me to go to the store for her and she gave me some money and I run home and give some of it to my mother and it makes her very happy so then I become happy and I go on through the day feeling very happy because I gave my mother some money to get something to eat in the house.

Even today I go to the store for the lady and she pay me good. I clean her yard and shovel her snow and get her paper ever morning.

THE
END

J.G. **Age 16**

IN THE MOONLIGHT

O, my brother lies dead in the night,
        and I watch him.
His corpse must be guarded from vandals
        and thieves.
The moonlight brings ghosts to his side,
        and I watch him.
The Devil lurks there in a bank of black leaves,
Watching my brother, and I watch the Devil,
Knowing my soul is the corpse that he seeks.
My brother lies dead, and I am my brother.
The moonlight shines on all.
Its water-light leaks over my face, upturned and cold.
Lifeless as I, who watch,
And He, The King of Corpses,
Who watches me.

Ralph Kenon **Age 15**

ALONE

When I go to bed I am alone. Sometimes I go to school alone. Sometime I play by myself. On Saturday Morning I look at t.v. and ate alone sometime. When I had a dog named Chase Sometime I walk. Sometime at night I really walk. Very alone.

Larry Green **Age 16**

MY BEST FRIEND

M. Baily and L. Hatch I like. Baily he is a nut and why I like Hatch is he a little devil. L. Hatch is always fight somebody he is devil. M. Baily is a little nut who wear glasses. He is 4 eye Cannon hard and he look like a worm.

Wanda J **Age 15**

I am trying to read what I see and not what I don't see.

funny!

Ronald C **Age 16**

My parents hardly never understand my problems because sometimes i will get in trouble like on April fool day. i would tell a teacher her toes are bleeding and then i'll get in trouble, when i would be only fooling around and then my mother would have to come to school and then I'll get a beating, and i'll try to make her understand it was a Joke like anyone would do.

One of the teaches in this school he's a man. When he be walking in the halls he would tap me on my shoulder and when i was in the 7th grade two years from now i tapped this teacher on the shoulder. I was just playing and he went down to the principal and tell them i gave him a CARATE Chop Chop and then i got in trouble right then.

My mother had to come to school and a lot of crap. And i tried to explain to her i was just playing with teacher. But she just didn't believe me. She think that i can't do nothing by myself.

Like another time Foster was at my house. He eats like a dog. One time i had to throw him out because he went in my ice box and ate a half a cake.

I was unable to verify this story. It was handed in without a signature.

HELPLESS, WHAT I WAS THROUGH

The Begining of this story began on feburary 10, 1966. I was at a party with my girl who was 16 & I was 13½. Then I saw my girl take out a needle. It was then that I saw the needle marks. I was so surprised that I didn't know what to do. She went into the bedroom. I followed half stupid at what I saw. I started to talk to her about the misstake she had made, but the dope was taking affect. I felt like dieing but no. I took the needle and I took a shot to see what would happen. It was painless. When my girl got up she tried to wake me up. But all I could feel were sexual affects. Then I woke up. I took 3 more shots and I was hooked. I needed the dope.

Unsigned **Age 14**

Walking alone around the park is just like forgetting everything. You see the free children playing. I remember when I was a kid and I always was playing and dancing with the other kids. Life is easier when you are small. The parents they care for you more and always gives you what you want. I wish I could be a kid again. They hug you and carry you. When they kiss you goodnight or sing a song to you. You get so sleepy.

P.J. **Age 14**

My dream is to be an artist. I know how to draw. I got talent. I will be happy is I know that in the future I will have my own studio drawing naked women. I love drawing faces and especially women faces. I love drawing figures.

I would like anything else. But I know that to do this is going to be hard to do. So I will be satisfied with a commercial art. Thank You.

W.N. wrote this poem while awaiting sentencing at Youth House.

W.N. **Age 16**

JAIL - LIFE WALK

Walk in the Day
Walk in the Night
Walk a chalk Line
Walk it right

Walk in the Sun
Walk in the Snow
Walk very
Wisely to go

Walk in the Mud
Walk in the Rain
Walk it easily
Without no pain

Walk on Water
Walk on a Leaf
Hardest of all is
Walk in Grief

Annette C **Age 15**

My best friend is my mother. She understands each subject I learn in school and helps me in each one.

She never slaps us. First she gets all the facts together. She asks questions, then puts the answers together and starts yelling. She understands about the way we do in school. She's very patient if she's in a good mood, but if she isn't, oh boy, will someone get hurt!

She's sweet, she plays like one of us, she's a good cook and keeps a swell house. Most of all we love her.

M.B. **Age 15**

FATHER

A father is love in the making.

Let's talk about father.

My father is one of the nices man on this earth. My father is a preacher. If you sit back and see how your father helped you, you will go into tears of enjoyment.

What do I mean by love in the making? Well your father is a protector of you. He loves you. Why he hits you, he is protecting for the future.

Let's talk about people without father.

Paul Parker **Age 15**

GRIEF

Grief is a gigantic snake ever squeezing until there is nothing, nothing at all left for your very soul to grasp onto. You lose track of everything that means something to you, you just know that you want to escape, escape into reality which in reality is not reality, your whole world revolves around it, it is a terrible experience, the only escape is to do something far beyond the comprehension of a normal person, it's like a drug, an awful terrible drug, your mind screaming with fear, screaming out for guidance out of the vast limbo, it's like heaven and hell, you're on top of the world yet your mind has a great burden.

The only escape is to do something to yourself, something that will hurt not only you but someone else as well, you must, it's the only way to find guidance out of this unreal world, this world of your own, and you emerge, you emerge ready for the world, you're a whole new Person, you're free, the world awaits you.

Arthur Jackson **Age 15**

I have felt lonely, forgoten or even left out, set apart from the rest of the world. I never wanted out. If anything I wanted in.

Unsigned **Age 14**

ME, MYSELF AND I

I writing this to let you know how I feel about everything around me, one first I hate flowers and the smell of them, I hate to go to funeral homes and look at dead people.

I like to be surrounded by guys and gals of my own and be hip and know whats going on around this messed up world. Everybody hates school, but I am different. I like school, I like to be where people are. I mean the teachers and hear them talk gibberish talk. I like to see and hear the kids own things and opinion on the crummy World.

Rodney S **Age 15**

FALLING ASLEEP

8:30 p.m. I was sent up to bed. I am not sleepy at all. The lights are on in my room, in the hall and in the bathroom. I smell my brother's cough medicine. I hear my mother and father talking. As I go up stairs, I can feel the wooden banister under my hands.

8:45 p.m. I'm washing up. The water feels warm against my face. I can see myself in the mirror as I wash. I soon hear my mother and brother coming upstairs.

9:00 p.m. My brother has a fairy tale book and he thinks he is really reading it. (He can't, because he is only six years old.) The lights are off in the bathroom, and in my mother's and father's room. I'm still doing my English homework and my parents are still talking downstairs.

9:12 p.m. I have just started yawning. My brother is crying because my father had to speak to him. I can hear the noise of the heaters in the house giving more steam. I can't explain the sound very well, except that it is the same as when a television set messes up. My eyes are starting to get watery.

9:17 p.m. I'm climbing into my bed. As I get into the top bunk, my brother is kneeling in the lower bunk singing the **Star Spangled Banner,** saying the Pledge of Allegiance and singing **America The Beautiful.**

9:30 p.m. I start feeling as though I don't ever want to get out of bed. My eyes are starting to get heavy. I still hear my brother talking to himself. The lights are still on in the bathroom and in my parents' room. The heaters are still making their noises.

9:40 p.m. My brother is now falling asleep, talking to himself.

9:50 p.m. My father comes up-stairs. The light is off in my room. My brother looks at the darkness and asks me, is it morning? The heaters stop making their crazy sounds. The house is quiet, everything is getting blurry. The last thing I remember is my hand hanging over the side of the bed and my brother playing with it.

V.B. **Age 14**

For what purpose was I born? I don't see.
To speak words that no one will listen to
No matter how loud I shout them?
To throw up dates, and events
just as I recorded them and be pronounced
a genius? To sit through school day after
day and be referred to as a "good child"?
To hear things that I shouldn't and then be
instructed to forget?

For what reason am I living? To see
man destroy each other, and we listen
to them preach godlyness and good-will?
To take things as they are and never question?
To live a clean life, only to rot away in your
grave? To have things your soul desires, prohibited?
To be told God is good, but disregard the fact
that the world—his so called "creation"
is bad.

But these are thoughts I must
not think if I am to survive.

David Warner **Age 15**

My Mother does things that nobody would do. She buys me and the other food. And she also buy me clothes. My Mother give me love. Sometime she help me with my homework. Before my grandmother died she helped me with my homework. I love my grandmother. My mother is good to me, But like all mother sometime it is yes sometime it is no. Who else is my Best Friend? "God," because God gave me my life. Not only me but The Whole World. He gave you, you and you Life.

So thank him.

OK?

Joseph L **Age 14**

THE WATER RACE

When I grow up I want to be
A big bold man to ride waves on a sea;
A man who swims an hour
Without getting tired.
And I'll go past the finish line,
I'll go right past it.
When I get my medal I will say:
"I've had a hard day."

Alvin and Robert wrote about how they looked to each other.

Alvin Robbins **Age 15**

ROBERT THOMAS

Robert Thomas is a boy who slants when he stands. When he walks, he walks with a bouncing effect. He is thin and wears glasses most of the time. He also wears braces on his teeth. His face is sort of thin and straight, his ears stick out from his head, but not all the way.

Robert carries a knapsack to school with his books in it. He talks with a sissing sound and sometimes stutters. He also blinks rapidly.

Robert Thomas **Age 15**

ALVIN ROBBINS

Alvin's eyes are black and his hair is blacker that black. He walks like a roach. He fights like an ant. He walks like a person who hasn't sobered up yet. His house is broken down.

High school student Frank Cleveland uses the pen-name "Clorox."

CLOROX **Age 17**

WHAT AM I?

I HAVE NO MANHOOD—WHAT AM I?
YOU MADE MY WOMAN HEAD OF THE HOUSE—WHAT AM I?
YOU HAVE ORIENTED ME SO THAT I HATE AND DISTRUST
MY BROTHERS AND SISTERS—WHAT AM I?
YOU MISPROUNCE MY NAME AND SAY I HAVE NO
SELF-RESPECT—WHAT AM I?
YOU GIVE ME A DILAPIDATED EDUCATION SYSTEM AND
EXPECT ME TO COMPETE WITH YOU—WHAT AM I?
YOU SAY I HAVE NO DIGNITY AND THEN DEPRIVE ME
OF MY CULTURE—WHAT AM I?
YOU CALL ME A BOY, DIRTY LOWDOWN SLUT—
WHAT AM I?
NOW I'M A VICTIM OF THE WELFARE SYSTEM—
WHAT AM I?
YOU TELL ME TO WAIT FOR CHANGE TO COME, BUT 400
YEARS
HAVE PASSED AND CHANGE AINT'T COME—WHAT AM I?
I AM ALL OF YOUR SINS
I AM THE SKELETON IN YOUR CLOSETS
I AM THE UNWANTED SONS AND DAUGHTERS IN-LAWS, AND
REJECTED BABIES
I MAY BE YOUR DESTRUCTION, BUT ABOVE ALL I AM, AS
YOU SO CRUDELY PUT IT, YOUR NIGGER.

Donald Morgan **Age 18**

I SPEAK IN AN ILLUSION

I speak but only in an illusion
For I see and I don't

It's me and it's not
I hear and I don't

For these illusions belong to me
I stole them from another

Care to spend a day in my house of death
Look at my garden are you amazed
No trees, No flowers, No grass, No garden

I love and I don't
I hate and I don't
I sing and I don't
I live and I don't

It all happens here in my room
And even it has me in an illusion

No where can I go and break these bonds
Which have me in an illusion

For I'm in a room of clouded smoke
And a perfumed odor

The heat rises and the window is stuck
And I broke the glass for air

Smoke and more odor fill the room
A quick and lasting black out

When I awoke only to find it was all an illusion
Next the lights dim to a haze which I can't see

Through a mist of air the perfumed odor has gone
By the tap of a finger the room brightens a little
Just enough to see
A shadow, a woman with long and dangly earings
She sits before me
A gypsy with long black hair and a rough face
And ghostly eyes

The gypsy has me in an illusion and won't let me go
And I speak only in an illusion.

Leroy Carter, known as Akmir, was born on September 19, 1948, and died on October 17, 1967. Here are two stories he wrote shortly before his death.

Akmir-U-Akbar **Age 18**

FROM EAST TO WEST

H.O.P.E. . . . The words which rang from the "Voice Box" . . . a word that meant freedom, peace and happiness.
Yes, with this I look upon the future without fear of failure, without fear of hungriness, nakedness or the out of doors.
Can tnis be for real? Is this happening to me?
As I retreat to shelter I wonder if this is the purpose, the plan of life I must live. Is it really the land I was meant to be in, the place I was to know?
I very much oppose this life. Yes, I'm getting out some way.

THE TRANSFORMATION

Working in a plastic corporation, day in and out I have grown weary of this automatic cycle of life. Problems arise when one must strain to produce new inventions in my type of work. Recently I was taken by surprise when a pile of synthetic type material fell upon me. Desperately trying to escape I found myself transformed into a pen.

Arriving at the assembly line I could feel a slight twitch in the refill of myself. I was being filled with ink. A metal point pushed up into my refill gave me an uncomfortable reaction. Just then a top was placed upon my head giving me protection from the constantly moving pens approaching.

To my surprise I was shipped and put onto display in my community and bought by my younger brother. Fortunately he took care of things that he had to buy on his own. And as long as I still can hold onto my reserved refill, my brother's hand shall be guided by me.

A boy in Youth House waits for sentencing.

Unsigned **Age 16**

FREE AGAIN

I would stay up most of the night because I couldn't get any sleep, worrying about going to court the next day, wondering what the judge is going to do or say to me. Wondering if he is going to let me go home, or will he send me upstate. I get up in the morning and take a shower and then the supervisor will be calling the names of boys who are supposed to go to court, and he calls my name. I go and get my clothing bag, change into my personal clothes, and then go downstairs and all of this time I am thinking of what is going to happen to me today.

After we eat, we go into a room, the room is 306. We wait. The time seems to go so slowly, and finally they call for the court people. We get on the bus and think all of the way through the long bus ride. Once we get there we go upstairs to a room and wait until they call for me. I'm so afraid because some boys are going home and some of them are going upstate. When time rolls around for the first bus to leave, they call my name to stay in court until they are ready for me. I sit and wait and wonder. Finally they call me. I am the last one to be called upon.

I'm sitting up in court. I feel sick to my stomach, because I am scared to death. The judge looks me up and down. Finally he said something to me and I answer him back. And finally, after about 15 minutes, because he has spoken to my parents, he said that I am paroled. A smile comes to my face. I leave the court room in a hurry. When I got outside I jumped for joy because once again, after a long period, I am free again.

C.B. Age 17

WHAT I HATE

It all started five years ago in the sixth grade. The teacher gave us an assignment to do and I was the first one finished so I thought that I would have some fun. So I drew a picture of a man committing suicide and I wrote that the man said that he was going to kill himself. And my teacher saw it and thought that I was going to kill myself. She gave it to the principal and the principal gave it to my doctor and he gave it to a psychiatrist up in New Jersey and the psychiatrist said that I was mentally disturbed.

Donald L **Age 14**

STORY WITHOUT A NAME

Once upon a time, there lived a little boy in a big mansion. He was only six years old, but he knew how to get food, cook and sew. For cleaning the house, he had one broom.

Sometimes, at night, he had horrible nightmares. He began to believe in ghosts.

The years passed, and soon he was thirteen. Now, when he went to bed, he had nightmares every night. Later he became very worried. He asked himself, "Will I be a madman?"

Twenty years passed. He was thirty-three years old.

One day, he looked in his mirror. To his surprise, his reflection had faded.

"Oh my," he said, "I am lonely enough!" That night, he looked in the mirror. His reflection was gone!

Just the same he kept getting nightmares. The very next week, he died.

Willy A **Age 16**

MY RAP

My story is all about my life.

When I was a littler boy my father was always beating on me and my brothers for just about anything we would do. We was living in Brooklyn then. And then one day he and my mother had a fight and my father had a very bad heart and he taked a over dose of pills and die in Brooklyn.

I didn't know what the youth house was.

And then we move to the Bronx were I met some new friends and start geting in a lot of gangs and start robbing places. And then I was lock up on May 6, 1966.

I went home and came back May 25, 1966, and stayed until June 30, 1966. And then they send me to a Star Camp and I get into two fights. And they send me back to the Youth House.

But when I go home the next time you can believe that I'am not coming back know more.

L.P. Age 16

WHEN I FEEL AT PEACE

The only true time I feel at peace is when I am asleep. Because I have no fear and no needs. I think sleep is the most closest thing to death so death must be even more peaceful. But you know what I very rarely feel like going to sleep. And when I do feel like going to sleep I don't feel like waking up. When I wake up I be very mad because I still feel sleepy but I can't go back to sleep.

And another time I feel at peace is when I am home looking at T.V. with no one else home but me and my mother. But don't let no one knock on the door or the phone ring. Because someone will ask me to come down and I become very disturbed. I bet I know what is going on in your mind this boy is sick in his head. But I bet you feel like this at times. You know what I just remembered I feel at peace with the pidgeons I used to fly but I don't like that peace because thats one of the reasons I am here now. So I am never going to fly birds again because they messed me up in life before.

I guess it's that some times I feel like being alone.

M.B. **Age 16**

DREAM

In my sanity (when I posess it)
  no dreams are permitted
I can coagulate my thoughts with
  the upmost precission
Coordination is perfect and my reflexes
  stream with a new found adrenalin

I despise dreams (fantisy that is.)
  For children with their
Imense maturity dream.
  (People in society don't dream.)
I want to be important someday
  (similar to those in high society)

C.R. *wrote these letters from New Hampton, a state training school, to Ed Grady, his former teacher at Youth House.*

Age 17

April 4

Dear Mr. Grady,

How are you and the family doing? Just fine I hope. As for myself, I'm fine, couldn't feel any better.

I received your letter today and was very happy to hear from you. Just to know someone cared made me feel like a real person. I had given up all man kind, and was going into a world of my own.

I haven't yet to hear from my people. I have received a money order, but no letter. Nothing telling me if everything is all right. Mr. Grady, I'm really hurt! This morning when they said I had mail, I felt good. Then when I read your deep letter, I felt like crying. I know someone in my family had a couple of seconds to put hello on some paper and send it off. I've been here going on two months now. But getting back to your letter, it was very touching. I don't know what to say. You're the only one who stuck with me. You're like a father to me. Mr. Grady, all the things you have done for me, I don't know how to thank you.

I shouldn't be telling you my personal problems, but you're the only one I can express my feeling to. I hope you don't mind.

So I'll change the subject for now. I finally got in Voc. Drafting, and taken it as a major subject. I'm doing very well in shop. Still trying to get in school. I'm planing on going to summer school.

By the way I would appreciate that shirt, size 18. I been wearing the same close since I been here, and I'd like to have a diary, in this way, I can keep a record of myself, and little things I say and do. (you know) I've been thinking and writing a book on my life. I wonder what would become of it, how many pages would I get?

So it's about time for bed in a few minutes. I'd like to see a picture on t.v. before time is up. So i hope to hear from you soon.

Sincerely yours

C.R.

April 21

Dear Mr. Grady,

How would the city be treating you at this point? Just fine I hope. As for myself, I'm fine but haveing a little troble with the fellas on my wing. A wing is a dorm.

I received the packages from you monday and was very glad to get them. Everything came in handy. Since I got the book hasn't any body been able to tell me anything (smile). I soupose to be a book writer.

I haven't yet to hear nor see my parents. Why I don't know. I'm sure it's not a money problem, because my parents both work, and my mother get's a little help from the city, which we aren't doing to bad for a family of sixteen kids. They sent my sister to school in texas just a few months ago. My older brothers and sisters work. I have a sister that workd in the post off.

Mr. Grady, do you know how I feel? Theres no reason for them to treat me this way. I'm human too. I understand you have kids to take care of and you can't play the part of my real father. Not saying I've gave you up. But don't you think it's wrong for me to look on you for my personal needs. You're the only one I can really express my feelings to. I've lost my girl friend. She gave me up! I mean, I have a child by this woman and if I lost her, I've lost all hope and dreams of ever becoming anything. I had my life planed out just swell. I was going all the way in Drafting. Now I don't even care to go to class. Before I couldn't wait for the next day so I could eat up everything the man was teaching.

But now look at me, a bum, and nothing but my close are so dirty it's funny. I can beat dust out of them.

I just wrote my mother a six page letter begging her to bring my close. I would have wrote you sooner, but I had to wait untill I could get a stamp, and the only reason I got that was, my friend had a visit and was nice enough to give me two.

So I'll change the subject for now. I don't like talking about it at times, because it makes me feel real bad.

So I'm very thankful for everything. What would I do without you Mr. Grady? Whom could I write to, when I write or think about you, my mind is put to ease.

So I hope I havent upset you or put you to thinking of me because I know you have more to do.

So untill the next letter is posted, I'm signing out.

Your second son

C.R.

April 29

Dear Mr. Grady

Thank you for your letter. I am glad to hear that you and your family are well. And I'm doing pretty good myself.

I hope you and your family had a nice vacation on Easter. Mine wasn't so pleasant, but I've come a long way without a Easter. So I won't let it get next to me now. (you know?) I didn't even notice where the packages was mailed from. I was so happy to get them, and to show off to my friends that someone cares.

The book was just great. I'll try and explain what happen with me and my book, on the next page.

2

Well, I was only writting every little thing down that had happen to me, for the few days I had the book. When the fellars on the wing got together and put a story together. They said I was takeing notes to give to the staff. So this went on a few days, and they findly made me stop what I was doing and put my book away. About 5 or 6 jumped me with chairs and brooms. So I had to stop writting in the book. But I still sneak and use it, but for another reason. I keep a record of letters I get and send, which isn't much.

(you see?) Mr. Grady I like to write. I don't know why but that's me. I like to try and put my feeling on paper. It seems more easyer that way, than to tell a person the truth to his or her face. Well anyway, book big or small, it was just fine.

About the shirt, you can tell your wife she has very good taste. Because the shirt was wonderful. I wore it to church sunday, and plan to wear it this sunday.

3

Mr. Grady; This is the pen you sent me, the one I'm writting with now. I hope you like the way it write's, cause I sure do. It write's so smooth.

Well, about my girl friend. I don't know. I guess she feels the same as I do at times. (like) I say to myself, why should anybody want me? I'm nothing but a jailbird. She didn't write and tell me it was all over, she just didn't write me back at all. I wrote her 5 or 6 letters asking her to forgive me for all my wrong doings, and I ask her nicely to write me, because I was so lonely without her. But it didn't work out right.

I don't think it was to difficalt for you to say anything helpful. You already have, by letting me explain my feelings towards her was good enough.

Well I think I've ansured your letter. Just swell. Now it depens on how you feel about it.

So if you'll kindly look over to the next page I'll try to

4

give you the outlook of my size and the colors. In pants I wear 32 x 32. In shirt, a large. Mr. Grady, you don't have to buy them new, I'll take some old close and will be very happy.

And if you'd like a few pictures of the things we do and how the place looks, just tell me how to use your camera. (I hope.) (Oh yea) I like royal blue for a color

So Mr. Grady, you've bought happyness into my life, how can I do the same for you? Just give me your wish and it will be granted. So please excuse this letter for being so short and all mistakes I may have made in it.

Sincerely,

C.R.

May 3

Dear Mr. Grady,

How are you and your family doing? Just fine I hope. As for myself, I'm fine couldn't feel any better, Mr. Grady.

I write to explain my feelings to you once again, but I bring the good feeling only. This letter will be short, because I dont know what to say.

Well I'm expecting my mother up this sat or sun. She called the people up and told them. I did just what you told me to. I wrote everybody in my family and I just knew that I would hear from someone. My sister wrote me and my girl friend came back to me. So I'm the happyest boy or man in the world today. (I think)

Sincerely,

C.R.

HOW I SEE MY NEIGHBORHOOD

HOW I SEE MY NEIGHBORHOOD

Most of the writing in **How I See My Neighborhood** is the children's attempt to understand the violence they see all around them. They want to know why their blocks are so dirty, and why they see so many drug addicts.

Rhonda and Lorraine are seven year old students of Naomi Hantz. They live in Brooklyn. Lorraine wishes ". . . they will stop killing people around my block and Rhonda's block. I keep dreaming I will get hurt."

Rhonda says, ". . . and I demand a Pretty good houses and more food to eat. that's what I demand and I better get it."

Carlos is also seven. He says there is too much fighting around his block, too much glass and food and paper in the streets. He says, "I like to people love each other."

There's writing about school, fighting, and criminals.

Throughout the section, there is the sense of imprisonment, of despair.

The last poem sums up many of the children's thoughts:

"You there, Mr. Yessir!
It's time to remember
It's time to see just who
You are messing with . . ."

Frank Campbell **Age 16**

THE SLUM

I'm walking in the street 116th, two in the morning all by myself. As I walk I fear—fear some crazy nigger is behind me, walking fast, faster I cross the street. As I cross I see a bunch of junkies in front of the bar and two lesbians making out in the gloomy tenament slum. As I pass the junkies I see a friend taking the stuff in his arm. I feel like scum. I sneer at the cops who don't care! The preacher who on Sunday is so "yes Lord" and just as high from a bag on Saturday night. I see the pimps on 116th street and Lenox telling the invader girl to get her blonde filthy ass back to 119th street and work. She begs him not to make her go. He kicks her. I see her and I spit, and inside I say, "goodbye you filthy whore"!

Later I'm on the bus, I vision the old man who slowly drops on his seat. I asked him "Are you tired sir"? He replies, "yes son, I'm tired. Working and living here all my life, giving all my money to the man. I'm old and half dead now."

The bus runs down 125th street. I see the stores, the stores where the man drains our money, takes it back to his family while we starve. I look up the avenue, I see the slums. I say to myself "I gotta do something. Stay and raise hell, or **GET THE HELL OUT** of here before I'm trapped just like the rest"!

Julio B **Age 17**

THE FIGHT THAT STOPPED FOR THE REST OF THE NIGHT

One day as I was walking to school, I bop into a kid. He said, "Your mother look like wolfman." So, I walk up to him and I said, "You're looking for a fat lip." He said, "Are you telling me or asking me?" "I'm telling you that your lip is going to be big as a watermelon." He said, "Why you little mother . . . ." I pick a date to fight.

The day came. It was on February 1, 1968 at 11:15 in the night. My boys were there. No noise around the area. Suddenly there he was and his boys. I jump up. I tell my boys to go when the coin flips. In a minute everybody started to run into each other. It was a big thrill to see my boys fight with other boys. Something went pck, pck. There I was lying down. I was stabbed. I was thinking if I'll die or live. Everybody ran, except my boys. My boys took me home. There the minute came I said, "Pete, Joe, John, Jr., Peter and two more boys," I said, "Goodby." 1:30, I was dead.

S.A. **Age 16**

WHY I THINK THE BROTHERS OF ISLAM IS GOOD ORGINIZATION

I think that the Brothers of Islam is a good orginization because of the fact that they teach you your true belief. The true god. And the fact that the black man is supreme. They tell you your true history about yourself. You get to know more about the true black mans history. Not what was written by the devil the fony White. But the true living god. You learn your reason for being on the earth. Its a very nice orginization to belong to. I can't express myself like I want to but I can try to given you a vague point of what I mean.

Like before I used to say that the black man can't succeed at nothing. But I have proven my own self wrong. By finding out the black man is the supreme people. That the first devil was a white mad scientist. I have found out a lot about the true black man through the brothers orginization. I can't express myself any better than this. I did my best. I have given you a vague reason why I believe the Brothers of Islam is a very nice orginization.

Allen L **Age 14**

As I be walking
Through the park,

I see little flakes of snow.

And when I look around:
I cannot see the wind.

Rhonda **Age 7**

I HAVE A DREAM

I wish that I could have a better block than I have Now. My landlord said that He was going to put Swings in my back yard. how can He do that When the backyard is junky I do not like people throw junk and I demand a Pretty good houses and more food to eat thats What I demand and I better get it.

Lorraine **Age 7**

I'M HAVING A TERRIBLE DREAM

I wish they will stop killing people around My block and Rhonda's block. I keep dreaming that I will get hurt. But that is not true. I keep saying to my mother I don't want to go out. But my mother says it is sunny out. I said that is not what's wrong. I'm scared that someone will hurt me.

Carlos **Age 7**

A round my block There is a lat of glass and food and paper and people fight all the time. I like to people love each other.

E.J. Age 13

ANGRY

When you get very mad at someone at a searten time, you push your lip out and roll your eye. Then you start picking on your little sister and brother and your dog and your friend. You do not want to eat your dinner.

Then you get mad at your self and you do not know what to do.

So you stop to apologize to your mother and father and your little sister and brother and your dog and your friend and you are not mad anymore.

Eugene Pitchford Age 15

DEATH

Last year in november my uncle was shot and killed.

They took all of his belongings that he had. The police don't have any idea who had done it. But who ever it was they will be caught.

He didn't have any enemies that I know of. All most everyone knew him.

The day of the funeral it was so quiet that you could hear a gun shot. It seemed like a sunday and everyone was in church. It was so painful.

Christopher Gamble **Age 15**

I HATE PIGEONS

I hate Pigeons because they're one of the dirtiest birds in the world. In Harlem where I live all you see is Pigeon shit, and it's so dirty. One day when I was in the fifth grade a bird (pigeon) was flying over me and a couple of seconds later some pigeon turd was on my shirt. Also in Harlem Pigeons just keep flying around you, they annoy you because they fly so low and just keep dropping it all over the place. If it was up to me I'd kick a Pigeon straight up its god damn ass just as long as they didn't shit on me.

Marilyn Aronson taught her children to write haiku. Here are three impressions of the ghetto.

Age 14

Snowflakes fall with grace
And cover city's dirt
Why do you leave soon?

N.T.

Little Bird alone
In a branch of snowy pine
Please do not be so sad

N.T.

Spring turns into
Summer my hate into like
And Fall comes once again.

Age 14

C.S.

M.B. **Age 15**

DEATH

It was death in my mother's friend's family. We were invited to the funeral. I was in my black suit. I was scared to death. The people were crying. Then the man said we could come up to see the man's body. My mother was pushing me up there. Findly we got up there. I was so mad that I push the man. I poke him in the eyes. I even pull his ears. Expect make-up to come off. Then the man got up and said, Hi folks. We were running for our lives.

The fat man was the first one out. Everybody was getting blocked in the door. The preacher jump out the window. He got hit by a truck.

We ran into the East River and drowned.

Unsigned **Age 15**

SEX

Most normal men are Notorious sex pots. Now boys is becoming intrested in it. They go around grabbing ladies asses and some just laugh because they like it. I'm intrested in it because I done it a lot with hoes. And if your intrested as to where you can find them 42 and Broadway. They make men pay but us boys if it makes them feel good maybe not. Their are lots around this neighborhood. I know because I've been living around here for a long time.

Unsigned **Age 15**

SCHOOL

I think school is alright but teachers are a drag. Schools and I don't agree. Sometimes I hate to get up in the morning. For what? To go to school.

Teachers don't understand how we feel. All is they no how to do is work work and homework.

I think if the teaches would take it into consideration that we are Humans, school would be much more fun. They treat us like dogs. I treat my dog better than what they treat us. Were computers and they just want to sink it into our heads but don't care how we feel. So are we to blame if the teachers are punks? They never kid around with us. As long as they get their paychecks they don't care.

R.W. **Age 17**

EYES SEE DIFFERENT THINGS

You would never recognize the old neighborhood today. Ever since you moved new buildings have been springing up all over. Remember the lot and the empty store next to your old house? Well, your house was torn down allowing the store and two lots to be combined into one large bowling alley.

Do you have anything planned for Thanksgiving vacation? If not, I think it would be great fun and even an adventure for you to see the old crowd again, as well as our much changed neighborhood. We could chip in and make our eyes blood shot. You will recognize some buildings, while others will be strange. You will also see old faces, some new ones in our crowd.

Can you spend Thanksgiving with us? You could arrive on Friday and stay until Monday morning. Our eyes can watch cars pass until they close. It will be a rare expreience for your eye to watch.

Magdalia **Age 7**

Your streets are too dirty and people throw things on the street. dirty streets are dangerous. cars come buy and kill people. you look two ways. dont look one way

C.G. **Age 15**

WHAT I WOULD WANT

The most important thing I would want are clothes because on my block the kids talk about the way I dress. But I'm in a city residence now and I'll start working January first. I'll be getting payed $7.50 a week plus a dollar each Saturday. And then I'll be buying all the clothes I want. I think in March I'll be going back around my block. By that time I'll have some of the clothes I want and my friends and other kids wouldn't have anything to say.

Thank you for reading this but dont feeling sorry because its all my mother's fault the way I dressed.

P.S. Although 7.50 doesn't do much I'll try to do and get what I can and even save some.

Unsigned **Age 15**

SOUNDS

Sounds can be curses or swares but are usually cunningly worded phrases that put down or rank-out somebody else.

The best kind of sound is a corny sound such as: "I went up to your house and asked for a drink of water and your mother gave me a bazooka and a hand-grenade and said . . . 'Good Luck' "

Mothers play an important part in sounding. I don't know why but for some reason mothers are the subject of all sounds.

Octavius Washington **Age 15**

Yesterday I was in the store. And then a little white boy came in the store and order some milk and a nigger. All the people in the store look at him. I said to myself, he made a mistake. He meant Hero.

But then agin he said "may I have a nigger." He was looking at me. No respect. No respect.

Terry J **Age 15**

I feel that dope addicts should be locked up behind bars. I wish this for the simple reason that many of the dope addicts on the street are strung out. (Up in harlem, we use the expression he's got a Jones.) Many of the addicts on the street will kill for dope. Others would rob for dope. The Women that are strung would sell their bodies for money to buy dope if you don't have the dope itself. That's why I say and know that they should be put in jail or put in a hospital until they can do without it.

Tim Engel **Age 17**

ON BROADWAY

Walking down to Broadway to get a compass for Math and a pack of cigarettes. At 90th on the N.W. corner there were a group of police cars and a few people gathered. Because people were involved, I went over expecting to see the remains of a fight. At first all I saw was a group of people, including cops, looking down. Then when I got closer I saw a very black Negro sitting down against Starks (Restaurant). Next to him were his crutches. One leg was stretched out and the shoe was falling apart. He was jabbering and crying incoherently. A strange feeling grabbed me—something was missing! Then I noticed—he had no right leg! One man was trying to make him drink a coke from Starks, while the stupid cops were standing around him talking.

He kept muttering, "They trahd to kill me, they trahing ta kill me, just like they did President Kennedy—they trahing ta kill me" and he kept sobbing and yelling, making feeble attempts at wiping off his drooling, which was all over his chin. One of the cops said, "We got the guy into a squad car but he said he wanted to get out, so he did and then he just fell." About ten people were there, looking at him while the man with the coke said, "I guess we better call an ambulance", as if he could think of no better way to get rid of him. Then the cop said, "I wonder why these guys always get drunk?" and another cop said, "They're all alcoholics anyway," Then the drunk black man started to vomit on his one leg and on the sidewalk. A woman bent down trying to clean him off and another woman laughed. I felt sick myself 'cause I was all mixed-up. A few minutes later an ambulance came and they jerked him up into a chair and I saw a big red gash beneath the kinkey black hair. A woman started to cry. Then as they were putting him in the ambulance a big man said to a cop, "He's been in there more times than the attendant has." They both laughed. I walked up to them on the street and said, "That's pretty funny isn't it . . . you dumb bastards!!" They both shrugged and started talking again. As the doors closed the man was still crying.

The straw of the coke was on the sidewalk next to the vomit. I watched the ambulance go away . . forever. I couldn't cry, so I took a bottle out of a trash barrel and smashed it as hard as I could against a dime-meter on Broadway.

Richard F. **Age 15**

LUNCH

My Favorite subject is lunch. What's school without lunch. Maybe we don't have a lot of time for it but its eating.

Lunch is a break between subjects to eat, sleep, play, and do homework.

Lunch is a break to settle problems with your friend. Lunch is chasing people, watching television or leasoning to the radio.

Lunch is buying and selling, horsing and yelling. I love lunch and without it I'll die. And whoever don't like lunch isn't eating.

At 12 oclock while others play ball, I eat lunch. While others yell and scream, I eat lunch. And now I can't wait til tomorrow to eat lunch. And before you know it, its the 6 period again.

Michael Benward **Age 13**

People are walking
To work they are going
Money money ha.

B.B. **Age 13**

In the noisy streets
I wait for a big red bus
To take me back home.

M.F. **Age 15**

I remember when this school first open, was a big drag at first.

Then about two months after the school open some kid tried to blow up the school. I know this boy, his name is Willie and about two or three weeks later caught these kids taking pot. It's geting pretty bad. Just the other day some kid asked me do I want to buy an "up". I know a boy he only 13 year old he believes in free love.

The problem with the school system is the teachers are to easy going and not enough power with the teachers.

A.P. **Age 14**

to day I saw a very butiful pigen. It white and grey. It landed on top of a fence I tried to grab it with my hand but it flew befor I could grasp it. I saw it fly off and it look butiful.

Terry J **Age 15**

THE PRINCIPAL

He is a no good son of a bitch. He's always talking bullshit when the truth is right. He thinks he's smart but he's nothing but a dum jew. When he talks to you he puts his stink breath in your face, and you could get high.

Ronald C **Age 16**

IN THE SUMMER

In the Summer you can go water skying in Central. the only thing you have to do is to get you self a tow and make sum fool go fast enough to ski. In the summer you can sniff the stink aire. You can go fore a train ride and when the trains get outside you can go to the back and pull the emergency clutch under the chair and the door from that car will open.

And then we sniff the poluted air. In the summer you can turn on the pump. You can spray the water and when people have there windours up, you make a home made swimming pool. An you can go and visit your relatives and then you come back and it's time come back rotten school. That's the wurst part about it when you come back to school. The same old thing.

Its awful the way these teachers make up lies, this is what sum of them write to Mr. Colaramo;

> Dear Mr. Colaramo i saw Richard Hudson in the Class sniffing his feet. He act like he was drunk. When he were finish he came in the Class and hit me over the head with a chair and slapped Mr Meyo over his bean head. That's all for now, Mr. Colaramo.

Victor Y **Age 14**

A SATURDAY

I'm in the Boy Scouts, we work and play. I'm patrol leader in my troop, it is one of my duties to do whatever the Scout Master says.

Two boys in our patrol did not got to overnight camp. It was very important for them to go because they had to pass their second class as boy scouts. For this they had to do their cooking and hiking outdoors. So the first thing I thought they should do was to get their hiking done. I said, "You can go whenever you are ready for me to take you," because that was one of my duties as a Boy Scout Leader.

They did plan the time they were going to go, but they did not tell me. Their names were Thomas and Cook. They came to my house early Saturday morning, I not knowing if they were coming or not. I jumped out of the bed, dead tired and said, "What are you doing here now?" They said, "We are ready to go on our hike."

Then I went on and got dressed. The boys waited for me. I was kind of mad but I kept on trying to be friendly.

We left for a hike to the J.F. Kennedy Airport. The two boys had their packs on their backs with the things they would need on a hike. We went by highways and byways. We saw people saying good-bye. I was still sleepy and we were not even halfway to the Airport. But Thomas and Cook went on as if they had just started. We were supposed to go there and come straight back, but we said, "We're already here, so let's look around."

Thomas, Cook and I went into the grounds, there were many buildings with different names; you could call it a station. We saw many intelligent looking people there. Big buildings and on the inside they were so clean, there was not a speck of dust anywhere.

We got a lift on a bus to other buildings, because the people knew we were in the Boy Scouts when they saw our packs on our backs.

After all the places we saw, we were very tired. We started home. I was even more tired: it felt like ten miles going back, when it was supposed to be five miles coming and going, two miles and a half each way.

We got home and I was never so glad. I fell right into bed. I said to myself, I don't want to see another airplane, building or anything like that for a long, long time.

Calvin D **Age 14**

THE NIGHT AT THE DRUGSTORE

In January when we had that snow storm, about nine o'clock, my grandmother did not feel well. So my brother and I had to go to the drugstore to get some medicine for her.

When we got outside it was snowing lightly. We walked five blocks to the drugstore. When we got into the store, a man with a black jacket and blue cap that covered his face stuck a gun in my brother's back and said to us, "This is a hold-up." There were six of them, four were dressed in brown jackets and dark green caps that covered their faces.

The one who stuck the gun in my brother's back told us to go to the back of the store. When we got there, the owner was on the floor. The stick-up men took all his money and then some things from the store. After that, they locked him, my brother and me in the bathroom. The owner told us we would have to wait for someone to come to the store and open the door. About fifteen minutes later a man did come.

Then the owner called the police, and I called my mother. My aunt answered the phone. I told her that the drugstore had been held up. Then she told my mother, and she said that they were coming to get us.

The police came and they asked us questions, and then my mother and aunt took us home. When we got home, they asked us what had happed, and were we afraid? We told them yes.

This is a real story.

G.P. Is a teenager who wrote this while in Youth House.

G.P. **Age 16**

CRIMINALS

As we know, there are a couple of thousand criminals in New York City. New York City also has a couple of thousand policemen, and law-enforcers.

Now, supposing there were no crimes, or criminals to be caught, in New York City, can you imagin how many people would be out of work.

Let's name a couple of jobs that would have to be given up;

1) police man (in uniform)
2) police man (plain-clothes)
3) detectives
4) builders of building for justice
5) judges
6) lawyers
7) steno-typers
8) guards in courts
9) secretaries
10) wardens
11) jail guards
12) directors of Youth Houses and many more positions.

Now I ask you, doesn't the criminal provide jobs for thousands? Therefore I feel that all criminals should be treated with consideration, due, to their advancement of industry.

T.B. **Age 8**

I was born in Brooklyn and in Greenpoint Hospital. When I was little my mother took me to the clinic to get shots. When I first start going to school I liked to wake up in the morning. First I lived at 341. It was a nice place. I had a lot of friend. In 341 everybody knew each other. There were a lot of riots. Once two men were fighting and one got stabed in the stomach. It's all right now.

Nell Moore **Age 14**

WHO LOOKS

Beneath the sidewalks
        to tunnels—
        merging
        separating—
        searching out the
                earthy blackness;
Behind the neons
        proving
        camouflage
        for purple-veined faces;
Past the faces—
        hiding
        selves.

Charles B **Age 16**

THE STORY OF MY BLOCK

I live in a block which is a bad block. It has dope pushing and pot smoking. In my building there are fights, killings and shootings. A man raped a woman on the roof and killed her. Another man stole a t.v., a hi-fi and some money; 500,000.00 dollars in cash. A cop ran after them. He fired three times in the air, then he said, "Stop! in the name of the law!" Then he shot the man in the arm, but they got away.

Two men stole some furniture out of a truck and they got away.

A boy fell off a roof and he died and his mother cried because he didn't listen to her when she said, "Don't fly your kite on the roof," but he didn't listen to her.

Nellie Holloway **Age 16**

LOCKED IN THE OUTSIDES

Here we go again, man,
I'm locked in the outsides of the white man's world
I hear them saying "We can work it out."
Yeah, they can work it out.
By giving us welfare and fixing the slums.
Of course, baby, how else
Listen to them laughing and declaring
"Give the niggers and spics some money,"
"Give them a shack to live in
And they'll be alright."
But don't pull tight, kid, don't fool me.
You! Boss man, you may
Give me a house and some bread
And I'll pretend I'm your perfect brother.
(A long time ago, huh
Old times and all that)
Now I want my share of the deal.
You live in the nice Park Avenue house,
While I slave to keep you there,
You wear pearls and diamonds
And I, costume jewelry.
Like they say, "A man' got to walk someday."
So it might as well be now.
Mr. Charlie is scared in his Bostonion shoes
And GGG suit
Now he hears about **Now.**
He hears, "Black Power, Baby."
Yea, Yea Black Power, **Now.**
Not tomorrow or Monday,
But now.
You there, Mr. Yessir!

It's time to remember,
It's time to see just who you are messing with.
Not your little pink lipped,
Black faced slave,
But a man and a people who are going to win.
Who are going to have power.
So listen, Mr. White Man, listen good.
You may give me some money
And a new house.
But a new house just don't make a new man.

THE WORLD OUTSIDE

THE WORLD OUTSIDE

"Since Men and Rats are the only beings that purposely kill their own kind, . . . what does that make us?"

That's one view of the **World Outside.** The girl who wrote it, Lucy, wants to know why people kill each other. Throughout the schools, children who are allowed to write freely are asking this question, over and over again.

Danny Goes to Doughnutland is a Kafkaesque nightmare about a boy who wanted all the desserts in the world. He finds that the outside world is a threatening place for him. Giant vegetables attack him and he has to run for his life.

One teacher asked her students what they'd buy with a million dollars. The answers ranged from amphibious jeeps to wigs.

One child wanted ". . . trees tall as giants," and another would buy "three lions, two bears, and a gorilla."

"Today is my day," begins one poem. "Today should be your day."

To these children the world outside is a puzzling place, as violent and threatening as the world within the ghetto.

Cynthia L **Age 15**

TODAY

Today is my day,
Today should be your day,
If it's your day and my day
It's everybody's day.
In your way is my day
Because you made a day that comes all the way.
And two days of a way equal today.
That will never fade away.
In our own way let's find ways
To make great exciting things happen.
In your ways, make my days,
You made a day that comes all the way,
And two days that are made up of your ways,
Those kind of days will never fade away.

M.B. **Age 14**

FATHERS

A father is love in the making.

Let's talk about father. Is father good. Some of them take, and some of them don't.

For instant my father. My Dad is a preacher. He is one of the nices man you can ever meet. I love my father. He is a charming young man and strong. To me he is helpful in many ways. A father is so good that you can't say it. There is no word in the world that can explain how a father is.

Claudia S **Age 14**

Lawrence of Arabia was an exciting movie. Every time I went out to get something to eat and came back to watch the movie, there was always some killing.

UNSIGNED **Age 14**

I think that women are the greatest thing that happen to man because men and women have the power to produce. And that all I got to say.

Jeanie S **Age 14**

One day in 1956, when I was six years old, I was in Baisley Park, feeding a big swan. I had two sandwiches, an apple, and a banana. I handed the swan the banana peel and that joker pulled me in. Ever since, I have been afraid of swans.

J.S. **Age 15**

DARKNESS

The sun goes down and the moon comes up. And children go inside. Friday night party begins. You go in and eat dinner. We sit down and talk about the things that have happened. Mother goes to the kitchen.

Father goes to bed and goes to sleep. My brother goes to do his homework. And here you are staring into the stars. It looks like the moon is a toy and the stars are little children playing on a blanket of black coals. And then the children go away, father and mother gets up and it's the sun. A new day is born. No more darkness.

Light sings all over the world.

J.M. **Age 16**

ANYBODY U.S.A.

I was the first man on the moon,
and believe me it's really made
of cheese 'cause I have Cancer.
And if you think they need us in
South Vietnam you are crazy.
Where do you think all this dope
is comin' from!

As for these foreign aid programs,
we can keep them. Those people
abroad need more than aid, they
need help! And if you don't
believe me, ask anybody in
Dead Patch, Kentucky!

J.M. Age 16

PROGRESS LIMITED

No trains stop here anymore,
and the old train station seems
to have become just a natural
part of the landscape.

The shutters look as if they are
cell doors, locking in our prisoner
the past.

The platform's legs look exhausted
from the long years of supporting
a building which we once called
progress.

But, just as the wind must cease
to blow, so must we cease to exist,
and eventually we become a natural
part of the landscape.

Richard F **Age 16**

GROWING OLD

One night my mother made me go to a dance with my friend and a old lady.

And when we went inside I felt like I was 65 years old. That place looked like a old folks home. There was so many old people there that it looked like a old folks convention. That dance was so old-fashion that Benjamin Franklin was there. And when I saw that I was so hot that the sun would look like a ice-cube.

And a other thing parents are always doing is (some of them) making kids wear clothes that is too old for them. An Example is my friend ("The Fox"). His clothes are so old-fashion that he'll make a old man look like he's a teenager. And his shoes, those things are so old looking that I hate to talk about them.

Juan F **Age 16**

How about people in a palace wearing luxury clothing? Many people eating and drinking rum till they cannot move. Ten slaves serving the food and rum. A big orchestra playing sweet music. I see a person throwing dollars to the air, like if he don't care that he lose his money.

Beside them many people without shelter, people hungry, people without clothes. People that have to work day and night and that they don't have enough money to support a big family. Children suffering because they have to work, helping their parents and their little brothers. People that need help and they never get it.

N.W. **Age 15**

Windy windy windy skys
deep blue fallen over my eyes.
The clouds so white
as the sun is bright
The sea is so blue in place
as the wind blows in your face
The birds so loud and clear
as if you feel a soft hand
in the air.

Susan Rosen teaches Junior High School in Harlem. She asked her students to write about what they would do with a million dollars.

S.M. **Age 15**

If someone gave me a million dollars for Christmas I'll get me a car with a motor and everything. Enough gas to go to the moon. Then I get a house in the suburban area. I'll have trees as tall as a giant and land to make everything look like the old times. Have a fireplace and a chair to relaxe in whenever I finish spending my money.

I get a bike, the fastest speeder in the world and a pool table. Then a color tv in my bed room and every room but the living room. Then I'll be able to get my brother a knit shirt so he'd keep his hands off mine. Then save a lot of it till I get the business of money in good hands.

Money is one thing in the world I'd like better then Girls. Money makes the world go round. When girls go and die on you money will live on and on. You know money is man's helper and keeps you out of trouble, I think. People can get their mother or girls some false hair. A good wig would make them feel good and make you have a little less money. You're not finish yet you have money in your pocket to spend.

Ronald C **Age 16**

If i had one million dollars i would buy myself the biggest house known and my own servents bringing my food up to me. I'd have one for everything.

Then i would give one penny to Charity an a nickle for unicef. With all the other i'm going to buy beer whisky wine. I'll give my Wife five dollars a month. I'll bail out every criminal I know.

I'll buy myself three lions two bears and a gorilla. I'll have 130343097 wives. The rest for College.

Francis P **Age 16**

if i have a Million Dollars I would buy me a 1943 military amphibian Jeep. And I will buy me a cashmere coat and a pair of gators at the shop and I will run for President. And I will be the first Black President. And I will buy me a 1968 G.T.O. and I will buy me a home for me and my love. And I will buy me a horse for my boy. And I will buy me a Mustang for my love. And I will buy me a million pack of cigarettes.

S.M. **Age 16**

Most of the time in Mr. Nesbit class we talk and crack jokes. Mr. Nesbit doesn't mind a bit. He'll say, talk now and you do it for homework. We like him because he is always playing with us and hitting us with the ruler. He punches us every morning when we come to school. He must like us or he'd never let us get away with things.

I'll write about Algebra just to finish this writing in good health.

Mr. Ryan is a good teacher or one of the best around, I would say, wouldn't you. Thanks for reading. I hope you liked it.

Donald L **Age 14**

DANNY GOES TO DOUGHNUTLAND

One gloomy afternoon, Danny Miller was having dinner with his mother.

When he saw that they didn't have any dessert, he asked, "Mom, why can't we have dessert, and have more of it than vegetables?"

"We can't have it, Danny, because sweets are not good for you", said Mrs. Miller.

When Danny heard this, he became depressed.

After drying the dishes, he did his homework. While doing his homework, Danny thought of the many desserts he could have. Cake, candy, ice-cream, soda pop, and expecially doughnuts. He loved doughnuts more than anything else.

When Danny finished his homework, he was so tired, he went to bed. Soon, he was fast asleep.

Suddenly, there was a gong. Danny immediately woke up. It was 12:00 midnight.

Then, there was a bright yellowish light at the window. Before Danny's very eyes there stood a man, all dressed in doughnuts!

"Who are you?" Danny asked.

"I am the man of Doughnutland", he said.

"How do we get there?" said Danny.

"We fly", he said, "by going across the golden stream, then the silver river, past the purple sun, the rainbow with gems, through the tunnel of fairies, and then we'll be there."

"Then", said Danny, "how do we get to fly?"

"We eat a doughnut," he said, "and we'll be there in two minutes."

So they ate doughnuts and immediately, they were there.

Immediately, Danny started eating doughnuts. They were delicious!

When he looked around, the man was gone! So he wandered further into Doughnutland.

As Danny walked along, he saw signs that said, "Turn back!" or "Trouble ahead!" but Danny didn't pay them any mind.

Soon he became so tired and full of doughnuts that he lay down to rest.

When Danny looked up, the sky was not a dark blue but a dark green, with doughnuts as stars!

The next day, Danny walked further, and in a courtyard, in front of a castle, he saw a lady.

The lady had on a long gold dress, with a pretty face and long golden hair.

"Hi," Danny said, "My name is Danny Miller."

"I'm Queen Mendal," she said, "but you are not supposed to be here."

Danny looked puzzled.

"The vegetables will get you if you don't leave," Queen Mendal said. "I guess I better go home," Danny said, "but how?"

"You just—", but before Queen Mendal could speak, there was a big rumble.

Danny and the queen turned to look. At the top of the castle, there were giant vegetables! Queen Mendal screamed and disappeared. Danny started to run.

Then all of a sudden, Danny found himself in the bed.

José **Age 7**

. . . and make peace too
and keep new york city good too
and make peace too and stop the
war toys.

J.M. **Age 17**

IT'S ALL IN THE WRONG PLACE

My mind holds this world in the
palms of its hands, and with
one single thought I can destroy
or turn it into a Garden of Eden.
I can mold it like clay into any
size or shape I want to.
I can open it and explore its
inners. But I, am like any man.
. . . . Handicaped. For this is
all in my mind.

I.J. **Age 13**

The first day of January, and every January first, is the first important day of the year because they make new dollar bills every New Year's Day. That's why it is New Year's Day. Every year they do something new.

J.L. **Age 14**

The silent snow falls
    In Central Park, while I wait
For Spring to slip in.

J.B. **Age 14**

The sailor watches
    His lost boat—quietly it
Slips from rock to sea.

Larry Brinson **Age 14**

BORED

Everybody in the world is bored at one
time or another. When people go to work
they are sometimes bored.
When they wait for trains.
When they wait for buses.
When they wait for lights.
When they wait for service.
When they wait for airplanes.
When children wait for school to be
    over with.
When people wait for the summer
    to come.
When they wait for winter to be
    over with.
When they wait for Christmas
    to come.

Benjamin Warrick **Age 15**

COLD

I do not like the cold
Because the cold can hurt you Just like yesterday I went to Jamaica Ave. yesterday it was very very cold We might have Frozen at the time. So me and Benge went on I was very very cold so cold that I wanted to go back home but I didn't.

So I went on in the store to purchase a toy. Came out I began to get cold again. bus came in the nick of time. I got on and all of a sudden I warm as if I was at my house so I start to take off my coat all of the people start to look at me I was very embarrassed so I got off at the next stop. and walk the rest of the way home.

Lucy L **Age 14**

There is so much unnecessary killing in our society. Our society is built upon killing or destroying others. A president or a "servant" of our government makes it to his official position by putting down or discrediting his opponents.

Hippie-ism isn't an answer to War, neither is Flower Power they are only escapes.

How many V.C. the U.S. kills seems very trivial when you compare it to auto accidents.

Many people believe that life is precious but if it is so precious why must we discriminate. Is it not as inhuman to kill a cow or a V.C. as it is to kill your mother or neighbor or fellow American.

Since Men and Rats are the only beings that purposely kill their own kind, and we exterminate rats what does that make us?

THINGS I CAN'T SEE OR TOUCH

THINGS I CAN'T SEE OR TOUCH

"Once upon a time there was a man whose name was Otis. He was a poor man, but he managed to survive." **Otis and the Doughnuts** was written by a boy who was in a class for the mentally retarded. The Board of Education once called these classes CRMD, and CRMD was what the children in the normal classes called their unfortunate schoolmates: Children of Retarded Mental Development.

As far as I know, Robert, who wrote **Otis and the Doughnuts,** wrote only this story. It's about a starving man's attitudes toward money and hunger.

In **Things I Can't See or Touch,** the children explore their ideas about death, sleep, love, science, sex, and God. Santiago says that in the days of the cavemen, ". . . the women united and went around beating up the men individually . . . This was the cause of love."

Jack W. disagrees that God is dead. He looked for God in the East Village, and found Him. "I found god a Universal. A thing in my heart. The feeling I can't rite about."

Carlos sees ". . . the sign of love trying to make its way through mankind. . . . Mankind is not as lost as it may seem. For there is a spark in those who think and strives. . . ."

A.O. doesn't agree. "Man will destroy himself and all with him," he says. A thirteen year old writes, "In a few minutes, I'll actually have a few minutes less of my life left than I do now."

The fables about **Adam and Eve, Why Man Has Nails,** and **Cavemen and Love** were written in Joan Blake's high-school class in Harlem. She asked the children to write about such maxims as, "the early bird catches the worm."

Most of them understood her, but one boy didn't. He wrote, instead, the admonitions he'd heard all of his life: "Don't put too much water in the rice. Don't put too much coffee in the water. You have cause too much trouble. . . . He is a bad influence on my boy."

This would-be fable belongs in the first section, **How I See Myself**, but it's in this section as an example of how a child's misunderstanding can be as revealing as his understanding.

Amalia had a pair of Good Glasses. With them she could see the Garden of Eden, full of ice cream and dress shoes. But she dropped her Good Glasses, and she describes her fall from a temporary state of grace.

In the poetry of some of the students like Carmen Martinez, Charles Franklin, and Donald Morgan, there are intimations of future greatness.

"Night. . . . To light a match in the mouth of the monster is to open a new sun," Robert S. writes, and Charles Franklin says of the **War Babies**, "They have no faces, They have no feet. They have no minds, They have no hearts . . . They have no world."

He is describing a world of hatred, but Benjamin Streater is thinking about love: "Love is an emotion. Without love this world be full of darkness and hate because love lighting up things."

Eddie Mayes Slaughter **Age 14**

When I was a little Baby my mother took me to a american Indian named Red Bell and she did not come back. He was a good man. When I was 18 I was a child of all Indians. And when I was 59 I was axed by a cowboy. I did not die then. But I heard my mother calling me and I am coming.

the
end

Herbert G **Age 14**

When I start to go to sleep
I get drowsy and see things
like little fireworks around me.

Nell Moore **Age 14**

Are fire escapes for
frightened people
crouching
ready
to creep
from
one inferno
to another

Louis Torres **Age 16**

THE EARLY BIRD

The early bird catches the worm. In the picture above the worm is caught by the early bird. Not always the worm get caught. Sometimes he is too fast for the early bird.

I think that sometimes this is not true because the birds are not always after worms, they might find something better to eat. One of these days the worm is going to eat the bird.

Robert M — Age 14

OTIS AND THE DOUGHNUTS

Once upon a time there was a man whose name was Otis. He was a poor man but he managed to survive. He was a quiet man but when it came to getting into a conversation, he could talk up a storm. It was because he seemed so quiet that hardly anyone ever talked to him. They just considered him a bum or a freeloader. Everybody thought he was stupid but really he was a wise man.

Well one day Otis was hungry because he had not eaten in quite a while. As he was wandering about, he happened to see this little donut shop. Just then he looked down and saw a shiny dime so he picked it up, went into the shop and took himself a seat. As he was waiting, he overheard a conversation that the waiter and another man were having. They were talking about a coin collection that the waiter had. Then the waiter came over to where Otis was sitting and said, "What would you have?" Otis replied, "One doughnut, please." As Otis was eating his doughnut he got an idea for how he could get some more to eat. After he finished the doughnut, he told the waiter how delicious it was. Then he exclaimed, "I couldn't help overhearing your conversation about your coin collection. It just so happens that I have a very rare coin and it will be all yours for some more of those delicious doughnuts." The waiter brought him two more and said, "Give me the coin." Then Otis said, "Just a couple more." Then the waiter gave him two more doughnuts which he quickly ate. Then Otis said, "These doughnuts are so good I can hardly stop eating them! If you'll give me just one more." As the waiter turned to get him the doughnut, Otis was gone. But on the empty plate was a shiny dime dated 1962.

Moral: To a bum, any coin is rare.

Wilfred G **Age 16**

WHY MAN HAS NAILS

In the beginning man found that he had little gray circles on the tips of his fingers. He didn't know what they were for, so he tried to use them in every way he could think. When he was nervous, he chewed on them, when he picked up a thin dime he used them. When he had an itch on his body he scratched it with his nails. And sometimes when no one was looking he even picked his nose. That's why man has nails.

Santiago S **Age 16**

In the primitive age, the cavemen would go around dragging their women through the growing grass and by their hair. Then one day the women united and went around beating up the men individually. The men then started copping pleas. This was the cause of love.

Jack W. **Age 15**

GOD

I see the Hippies wearing buttons saying "God is Dead."

And I disagree with them. For only mortals are born and Die, but God isn't a mortal.

I have seen the other side, the evil. Believe it or not, I had meeting with a African Warlock. He shown me ther was evil. So I said thier must be good. So I set off looking for god.

I went to a book store and I read a Book on Mehar Baba. For he was god, god had entered his body, just as god had entered the bodies of Budha, Jeasus, Mosus, and now Mehar Baba.

And after reading his teaching I found god a Universal. A thing in my heart. The feeling I can't rite about.

Benjamin Warrick Age 14

DEATH

It was the day after Xmas. My brother and I went to the cleaners for my mother. It was wet that day because of the snow. His pants was very very wet, so after we got to the house he started to clean his room. After he got his room clean my mother told us to go in one of the rooms but we did not have a room to go to, so we went in his room but he didn't want me in his room.

I went in there anyway. So we got into a little fight. We was not hitting each other. After a while of that he went to my mother and told her that I was bothering him so she called me and I did not come so she stopped calling me. He started back to the room when all of a sudden we heard a loud noise. Me and my sister came out of the room. There on the hallway floor there was Joseph Warrick, my brother. On the floor around him was a puddle of blood and his eyes were rolling like marbles in his head. So my mother came running out of the kitchen.

When she got there she asked what had happen but we didn't know what was wrong with him.

So my mother and my sister picked him up and put him on my bed and took off his wet clothes and put on some dry ones.

And a few hours later some policemen came and took him away. That the End.

Eddie Mayes Slaughter **Age 14**

OLD OLD PEOPLE

What will I do when I become an old old man? I do not want to became an old man because when you become an old old man you are next to death and want to live foreever.

I Hate death. Life is no good to me if it ends with Death. Some old old people welcome death. I do not, so I do not like oldness.

Jose C **Age 16**

Jose is retarded and when I knew he was retarded I took him to the retarded hospital and they give me $100 for him. The doctor said he sure is retarded and Thank you.

Clorox — Age 17

REJOICE

REJOICE CHILDREN, LITTLE BROTHER, HE'S DEAD.
WHY, THAT'S THE BEST THING THAT COULD HAPPEN TO HIM
'MEMBER HOW DARK HE WAS WHY, HE'D NEVER'VE GOTTEN FURTHER THAN HIGH SCHOOL.
HE COULDN'T PASS LIKE YOU DO RODNEY. . . .
SO WHAT, HE WAS ONLY TWO YEARS OLD.
NOW HE'S GONE,
THERE'S MORE FOOD TO GO ROUND.
RATS GOT TO HIM IN HIS CRIB AND THEY HAD A FEAST
NOW I CAN GO BACK TO SCHOOL AND PLAY IN THE AFTERNOON.
'CAUSE I DON'T HAVE TO BABYSIT.
DON'T HAVE TO PAY NO MORE DOCTOR AND CLINIC BILLS: CAN PAY MR. GOLDBERG ALL THE BACK RENT ON THE APARTMENT.
MAYBE NOW HE'LL FIX THE FALLING PLASTER, LEAKING TOILET BOWL, AND GIVE US A NEW STOVE AND ICE BOX.
YEAH BROTHERS AND SISTERS, I'M SO GLAD LITTLE BROTHER IS DEAD.
HE DON'T HAVE TO GO THROUGH WHAT WE HAVE.

Randy is seven, and in the second grade in Brooklyn.

Randy E **Age 7**

I HAVE A DREAM

Dr. Martin Luther King was a great man.

He tried to help all the poor black people. And he was going around tring to help black people and white people to stop fighting so much. And when I heared that he got shot and died I felt like cring.

And I had a dream that he was in my room laying on the bed and it was dark in the room. And I'll never forget it as long as I live. And I think the man that shot him should be put in jail.

And I bet he wanted to stop the War in Vetnam after he was finished with his other work to. I saw his funeral on Saturday. And I don't see why Black people and White people can't be friends. We are all made the same way inside so why can't we be friends? But I see that Black and White people were at his funeral. But I'll never ever forget it.

the End

Carlos A **Age 15**

LO, THERE SHALL BE AN ENDING

Lo, there shall be an ending to those who think and strives on there mortal thoughts. Though I'm really a mortal, my thoughts proves otherwise. It hath come to my attention that those who dwells upon this bewildered planet are in need of something to bestow their confidence and mortal souls on. These mortals are in an advancement of science and social life, but I see greed, hatred and jealousy towards their fellow companions. Though this is all true I see the sign of love trying to make its way through mankind. Not that they seek to overlook there petty troubles, for man does not woelly seek a solution. It is not for me to judge the mortal race, but through the ages the covenant of breaches hath been reached and the realm eternal invaded. Mankind is not as lost as it may seem. For there is a spark in those who think and strives and there in a time might ignite and illuminate the universe. I hath spoken!

Craig S **Age 16**

THE DOWNFALL OF MAN

Man is a destructive machine.
he operates on human beings.
he lives in a world of brains and
money,
And his every day is bright and
sunny.
But the poverty-stricken and the
mentally insane
Bring no troubles to the man with
the brains.
So when the big man starts to
rise,
The rest of Humanity will up
and die.
Then when the big man's heart is
in pain,
They'll wish they could start
over again.
But not only will they wish and
cry,
But soon thereafter they will die.
Then when the earth is dust and
sand,
That will conclude the downfall
of Man.

Augustin O **Age 15**

SOMETHING OFF MY CHEST

I'd like to get something off my chest. It concerns religion and Science. Since the begining of time man has had some form of religion. It is my opinion that in the foreseeable future, their will be no form of religion on the face of the earth. This opinion is because of one major obstacle **Science.**

Science has begun its deadly task of tearing down all form of religion. It does this by contradicting the basic (socalled) facts of religion. The theory of Evolution is one of these points. The thought that man has evolved from a fish destroys a young person's belief in the first men and women. In this age where man himself is making miracles, where should I turn? I'm torn by Religion and Science. Which way should I turn. Are we, too, worshiping just idols like men of the past? There is one thing I am sure of, if there isn't an all powerful hand, if the almighty is but another god among gods, the fate of man is obvious. Man will destroy himself and all with him.

Unsigned **Age 16**

WHY DID EVE GIVE ADAM A PIECE OF HER APPLE

One day Eve came upon an apple. The apple was gleaming in the sun. She looked at it with big eyes. She ran all the way to where Adam was and said Adam come to see my apple. So they went. She said "Adam would you like a piece of my apple?" He said, "No." "Adam, if you don't take a piece of my apple I won't give you a piece of myself."

This boy misunderstood the teacher. She asked him to write about a maxim such as, "A stitch in time saves nine." Instead, he wrote about the admonitions he'd heard all of his life.

Walter P **Age 16**

Don't put too much water in the rice.

Don't eat too much chicken on Sunday.

You have cause too much trouble in this neighborhood. Early to bed early to rise, makes a man healthy and wise.

Don't put too much coffee in the water.

He causes too much trouble in the neighborhood.

He has only live in the neighborhood 6 months and he has cause trouble with all the youths and all the adults.

Benjamin Streater **Age 15**

LOVE

Love is a warm thing. Love is an Emotion. Without love this world will be full of darkness and hate because love lighting up things.

Curtis M **Age 14**

THE HOPELESS TREE

There was a man waiting under a baby apple tree. He was waiting for an apple to grow on it. He would just sit there and wait and wait but it never grew. He watered it every day but it just didn't grow. No matter what he did, it did not grow. So the man got discouraged and gave up hope for the tree. He wanted to cut it down. So one day he dicided to do it. He said he would do it on a Sunday afternoon, rain or snow. So on Sunday there was a fog and he could not see the tree and so he did not cut it down.

The following Sunday a baby apple was hanging on it.

M.B. Age 15

A LITTLE STORY ABOUT WAITING

The turkey walks in the kitchen not knowing the thing that will happen. He walked in and got cooked and the chicken still waits.

The chicken said to himself when the turkey got lost in the kitchen,

"I'm waiting all day long, wondering if my friend will ever come home."

A turkey and a chicken were good buddies. They were walking down the street doing nothing.

It was a street with lots of stores and restaurants. They finally came to one where something smelled good. The turkey wanted to see what it was. The chicken only went up to the door and said, "I'll wait for you."

The turkey went in and the closer he got the better it smelled. As he got real close he flapped his wings, the smell of the turkey was so irresistible he had to go right into the kitchen. As soon as he walked in, the chef closed the door, which proves two good-smelling turkeys are better than one.

Robert S Age 15

NIGHT

Night my third fear. And the first fear for some people.

When you say night you think of ghost, witches, and monsters. But when I say night I think of magic.

As I sit here I look out my window and see the vast, monstrous darkness of night and I think how the people in the old day of yore felt. With there magic poshents and there crystal balls.

I wonder what they thought when they look into the sky. Could they ever dream that some day a man will fly into the deepest night.

Night, Night, can man beat it or live with it all their lives. Some people love it. Some hate it. Some are born in it and some die in it.

I know I could not live in night. Id have to die in it. To light a match in the mouth of the monster is to open a new sun. You sometimes think that it is a man, that talk to you when you enter it. But I say it is a shadow that falls only on the ungodly. And destroy the unrightest.

Benjamin Warrick **Age 15**

Night is a thing that comes and goes. Just like yesterday at the sun going down. It was day. Next I looked it was getting dark and darker. So then I started to get scared and I went to my room. Started getting ready for bed. Then I start hearing a noise like someone was trying to brake in. Then I put my head under the covers. Then all of a sudden they stop. I got up and got my stick, and started for the door. Then the sound went away again.

Michael B **Age 15**

DARKNESS

Darkness is a cloud, a dark cloud formed in us. We live in a world of darkness.

There are two kinds of darkness, maybe three kinds. There is a darkness out the door, that's not important. But the other one is important, the darkness that is in some people, the darkness of people who are blind. Darkness is not a part which they can't see, it's the darkness. We can see some people walk in darkness almost all the days of their lives, we call them blind. They have never seen light.

Darkness is just like fear. You are afraid of a dark spot in the house where you lived five years.

Some are afraid of darkness and can't see the other.

People walk down Darkness Street the same as Fear Avenue.

Alvin M **Age 16**

I would like to stay in the bathtub for the rest of the afternoon, or else I'll see television and play cards with my brothers. Also I would try to keep in a comfortable place, where I could feel the cool breeze and relax, but most of all what I wrote is not true, because I would be working.

But usually on sunny days I am locked up in the house busy, because my mother doesn't like to go out. On a sunny day, I would like to go to a lot of places and just waste my time until dark, walking, singing, playing, and most of all eating at the same time.

Maybe on a good day like today I would go to my aunts house in Brooklyn or to my other aunts house in the Bronx or else I would go to one of my favorite schools, and visit some of my teachers or I would go to the seminary where my big brother studies at, because it is a nice place to visit and you could smell the pine trees air.

Frances **Age 15**

NEW YORK

New York is a dirty filthy place to live. It is full of dope addicts, pot smokers, speed and LSD and nothing is being done about it and I think it is disgusting the way the kids are losing their lifes from sniffing glue. I just think it is disgusting.

Amalia G **Age 14**

WHEN I WAKE UP IN THE MORNING

When I wake up in the morning I had a pair of Good Glasses. I saw a woman and she told me her name was Miss Gilbert. She brought ice cream and a lot of things like dress shoes. I also saw a angel in the sky. She help me out with things. She told me to imagine what was in my head so I said a lot of things like Candy, ice-cream, cake also childrens playing with toys and dancing.

But then I drop my Good Glasses and when I pick my Good Glasses up they had bad things written all over them. I saw that Miss Gilbert took all my Good that she gave me, and the Angel turn into a monster and my ice cream melt. My shoes had a hole, and the sky turn into smoke and my cake disappeared before my very eyes. I liked my Good Glasses.

Dennis N **Age 14**

I like to lay in on my bed looking up at the stars. I wonder what is really out there. I wonder if there is life on any planet in the entire unaverse. And if there is I wonder if they would understand us. Many people say they do not care what is up there. But if they seen and understood them and learn the things they know, I wonder if they would really say alright let's go to the planets and the galaxy and constellations.

This what I think about. I guess you do not understand me and the way I think. Some people say I am a nut. Well if that's what they think I do not care what they think. I know only what I like and do not want anyone to make me think different in any way. I guess I like to think about the stars.

D.M. Age 14

MY LIFE AS A SIDEWALK

One day, it was one of those hot summer days. I was laying down beside the street and I did not tell you that I was a sidewalk. It was on a Saturday. I can not remember if it was in the morning or the afternoon. So let me get to the story now.

Everybody was busy walking on me and I was trying to get a sun tan. I was very mad. I almost started to blow the people off, but I started to think of the people that made me a sidewalk. So I said to myself in the night I will get my suntan. But then I realized that when the sun goes down you can't get a tan.

Then I blew the people off of me and from then on they did not walk on me again and I got my suntan at last.

Unsigned **Age 15**

For some odd reason on Christmas I have bad luck. The only part I like is getting away from the teachers that punish you so much for nothing. I wouldn't want any expensive thing because your friends get jealous. I'd wish I had a father and a real mother. I don't want to live in a mansion because people are ready to rob you. Right now I am alright the way I am.

This is a letter from a 2nd grade child written the day after Martin Luther King, Jr. was killed.

Age 7

Dear Mrs Hants
I hope you never never
never never die.
From Diahann

April 5, 1968

Ronald C **Age 16**

My favorite subject is lunch, not because of the food. If you go walking around you see people eating garlic sandwiches. They even put grapefruit juice in their potatoes. The food they serve is usually nasty. It's half cooked and dehydrated powdered steak and eggs. When you walk through the rows you see people flying milk and runaway plates. CG be the first one down there. When they coming down you'd better get out of the way if you don't want to get stamped. They're like wild gorillas. That's why it's CG. Crazy Gorilla.

The best thing to me is what they serve is it's chopped suey. Mr. Bemaurin always be down there. He's always beating up somebody but he never do it to me. He kicks people without no coat. Some people take off there shoes to sniff there feet and Mr. Bemaurin throws them out without they shoes on. He's a big butcher. Richard Brown he go around the lunch room taking everybody's lunch. He takes mostly the powdered milks and dehydrated steaks.

S.M. Age 16

GROWING UP

Growing up is a problem for you and your mother. The things I had to do when I want to avoid a beating! Like saying please, thank you, you're welcome, yes, no, things like that can drive you crazy. I feel that you can grow up without the proper way to talk and act.

But, it was worth it in my wonder years when I was in the ages of 1-12. Now, I think I know the meaning of right and wrong. When you grow up the years seem wonderful for a while and then you seem to get along alright one day, and the next you're in bad shape.

The higher you get in life the more you want to know about things. Like the facts of life, which your parents talk about the birds and the bees. By now you are mature enough to date girls, go out to dances and enjoy yourself. Then after a while girls will mean more than a kiss on the hand or a handshake. You will develop the sense enough to take the girl out and give her a good time. Then if you have the feeling you can't let go of her, invite her to your house and get tight with her and if you are still in the loving mood, you will date her more than you have in the past.

Now, some of you who read this will say, that don't make no sense to go out with girls, they're a waste of time. If you don't get your rap together and fast, you're going to go through life with a dog.

Now that I'm finishing, I something to tell you. I love girls and now some love me. Then if you ever are happy with a girl try to keep it that way. Because, girls are the seeds of our civilization and don't you forget it.

Arthur Jackson **Age 17**

SLEEP

Sleep is a dark dimension with an automatic movie projector which cuts itself off and on by a subconscious switch.

Unsigned **Age 13**

When I was younger, I really had a strong fear of death because of such sudden deaths of my relatives or friends. Now my fear has somewhat lessened and yet somewhat increased. I often look in the mirror and say to myself, "In a few minutes, I'll actually have a few minutes less of my life left than I do now." Everyone is constantly saying that "You're young. You have a big life ahead of you." This kind of thing is very easy to say to someone else but I don't think that anyone can really look at life that way, at least I can't.

Often, I'll be in my room doing homework, when my mind will just wander and I think to myself, "I'm growing old so fast and there's no time in life to really do anything." When I think back 5 years ago, when I was 8 years old and I can remember specific incidents and specific things that people have said to me I somehow can't believe that it was 5 years ago when it seems like yesterday.

W.A. **Age 14**

DEATH

My name is William, I died 2,000 year ago.

I wanted to live and I was too young to die, but I had to go some time, so I was walking in the wood and I fell into an open grave. I was down there. A wino was coming home so he said, I think I take the short cut home. He was walking through the graveyard and he heard somebody say, it's cold down there. So he looked around, he said no wonder you cold, you kicked all the dirt off.

the
end
thank
you
and
happy
death and night

Carmen Martinez **Age 17**

MUSINGS

Take hold the crutch you lame believers
Limp through life upon the sacred word.

Yours is but to forsake all known truths
Forsake your legs, forsake your reason
Wonder not how you'll stand it through life
The cross supported Jesus once
And likewise it will do for you.

This life is but the road to that other
That which is ashes, that which is nought.
There at that to which you have aspired
    To thee new legs will be rewarded
    Stronger, perhaps, the Lord only knows.

Take hold the crutch you lame believers
Limp through life upon the sacred word.

Donald Morgan **Age 18**

A POEM

BEAUTY TRIUMPHS IN THE END OF MAN
SPEAKING OF HIS DISORDER
HURTS THE SILENCE
UNDER YOUR BODY
LIVING IS DYING AS BEAUTY
MOVES
THE ONE DARK AND ONLY
THING
THE END OF SUNRISE AS THOUGH
IT WAS THE WILD LIVING
WHOSE TENDERNESS IS THAT OF
THE STARS
HEAVY AS AIR MIST
AS PAIN
FAITH FLIES
ON A LIGHTED ONLY NIGHT
THEY ASK FOR VOICES THAT
ARE NEVER HEARD   OF DYING
WHOSE LIVES ARE MYTHS FOR
THEIR SOULS
ALONE   PUT TOGETHER IN DRY
BODIES AT THE BOTTOM OF ITS
PEAK
WHO HAS PASSED AND WHO HAS
GONE
WHOM YOU SAID TO BE LOVERS
THIS SILENCE MY BROTHERS
THEIR BODIES ARE NOT
UNLIKE THE DARK DAY'S LIGHT.

Charles Franklin **Age 18**

A POEM

Another man has died.
Give away his clothing to relatives.
Lying in wait beneath the oil furnace.
Under the cellar steps
Cowering from sight behind the
shower curtain.
Give his money away,
To the casketmaker;
To the priest;
To the garbageman;
To the slut in his bedroom.
Sell his house and his land.
To the church . . . looks good on
the record book.
Sell his children into slavery,
Claim his wife;
Fire up the ovens for his body,
And bury his soul in the ashes.

Charles Franklin **Age 18**

"WAR BABIES"

I saw them again last night,
Down by the railroad tracks.
Playing in the twisted rubble.
Sleeping under a bent ironing-board.
Bleeding in an abandoned truck.
Crying in a fresh-dugged grave.

I walked down by the sea,
And saw the little bodies floating
Out with the tide.
Watched them stumbling down
the sands on broken stubs.
Looked in a cloud and saw them cough.
Screamed when they held their
arms to me.
Sobbed as they crawled away.
Cried as I watched them leave.

They have no faces,
They have no feet.
They have no minds,
They have no hearts . . . . . .
They have no world.

Donald Morgan **Age 18**

A POEM

WHAT HAPPENS TO LIFE

WHERE DOES IT START, BIRTH
WORLD KNOWN TO BE BEAUTY
THE BLOOD DRIP BY DRIP
MAKES IT ALL SEEM A LOSS
WHAT HAPPENS TO LIFE
        CAUSED BY BIRTH
WHERE DOES IT GO OR END
WHAT BEAUTY IS LEFT
MORE THAN EVER DEATH COMES TRUE
IS THIS THE END OR
I ANSWER ONE QUESTION WITH ANOTHER
CAN IT BE BIRTH HAS NO END
DRIP BY DRIP
BLOOD FLOWS
LEAVE THE BODY DRY
TO BE THE END
WHAT HAPPENS TO LIFE
DOES IT DRY
LIKE THE MELTING OF SNOW
IN WINTER
OR LIKE A RIVER DRIED
BY THE HEAT OF THE SUN
IN THE SUMMER
DOES IT START ALL OVER
AGAIN IN A DIFFERENT
FORM
OR DOES IT JUST DIE?

AND NOW . . .

What will happen to these children, and to children like them all over America? That is the logical, the tragic question.

The answer up to now has been: Nothing. Without any further encouragement, they will remain trapped in the ghetto, trapped by a system with its fingers in its ears.

I hope that this anthology helps to change this bitter reality, for these children have so much to say.

These are children's voices from the ghetto. In their struggle lies their hope, and ours. They are the voices of change.

ACKNOWLEDGMENTS

First, my thanks go to the children. It is their book.

Also, my thanks go to Marilyn Aronson, Gregory Armstrong, Elaine Avidon, Joan Blake, Beth Gilbert, Ed Grady, Spenser Jameson, Naomi Hantz, Eve Greenspan, Naomi Levinson, and Susan Rosen, all of whom made this book possible.

Thank you, Elizabeth Slater, editor, typist, and friend, for all your devoted help and concern.

Some of the writing in this book has previously appeared in **What's Happening** magazine. Elaine Avidon edits this journal of New York City ghetto children's writing. Subscriptions are available at $3.00 per year from **What's Happening**, Horace Mann-Lincoln Institute, Macy Annex Building, Columbia University, 120th Street and Broadway, New York, N.Y.